KARINA GARCIA'S
NEXT-LEVEL
DIY SLIME

BuzzPop

This book is dedicated to my supporters who made me who I am today. Let's get slimin'.
-KG

BuzzPop

An imprint of Bonnier Publishing USA
251 Park Avenue South, New York, NY 10010
Copyright © 2018 by Karina Garcia
Text by Aubre Andrus
Additional photography on page 79 by *Life with Brothers*.
All rights reserved, including the right of reproduction in whole or in part in any form.
BuzzPop is a trademark of Bonnier Publishing USA, and associated colophon is a trademark of Bonnier Publishing USA.
Daiso is a registered trademark of Daejang Industrial, Ltd.
Elmer's Glue-All is a registered trademark of Elmer's Products, Inc.
Lucky Charms is a registered trademark of General Mills
Etsy is a registered trademark of Etsy, Inc.

Manufactured in the United States of America VEP 0518
First Edition

10 9 8 7 6 5 4 3 2

ISBN 978-1-4998-0799-8
buzzpopbooks.com
bonnierpublishingusa.com

KARINA GARCIA'S
NEXT-LEVEL
DIY SLIME

slime

noun | \slīm\

1. an ooey-gooey substance you can make yourself

    a. otherwise known as gack, flubber, goo, or putty

2. a DIY craze that's taken over social media

3. a personal obsession of YouTube star Karina Garcia

slimer

noun | \slīm-ər\

1. a person who makes slime

    a. for example: you!

Main Ingredients of Basic Slime

- PVA (polyvinyl acetate) glue
- Baking soda*
- Contact lens solution*

*Most typical recipes for slime contain borax, but due to consumer concerns, Karina substitutes baking soda and contact lens solution for borax in her methods.

CONTENTS

INTRODUCTION

The slime community has expanded so much since I wrote my first *DIY Slime* book. We were just starting to experiment with different types of slime—clear, crystal, edible—it was just the basics. Then, slimers like OG Slime, Anathema Slime, Peachy Bbies, Fluttershy Slimes, and so many more took it to the next level with butter, fishbowl, jelly, and cloud slimes. Now there is a slime for everybody.

If you haven't tried playing with slime yet, try it! I have not heard of a single person who has tried slime and thought it was boring. Even my dad likes slime!

I'm personally obsessed with really thick, soft, glossy slime. You can poke it and make noises with it. I can play with it for hours. It's really therapeutic.

These days, slime is literally flying off the shelves. Online slime stores are selling thousands of containers per week, and many types of it are selling out within minutes. Even my fiancé has his own slime shop. So if you get really into making slime, you can think about making a career out of it.

Use the recipes in this book as jumping-off points for your own creations. It all starts with a basic slime recipe, but whatever you add from there will turn it into something next-level.

Add some sparkles to give it a mermaid twist, add different colors to make it into a snow cone, or add a really cool scent to make it a whole experience. Take it slow, follow the directions, and experiment! You can always add stuff to fix slimes gone wrong:

TOO STICKY: Add more baking soda and contact lens solution.

TOO THICK: Add hot water or skin lotion to make it softer.

TOO MUCH A TOTAL FAILURE: Try a different brand of contact lens solution.

One thing to note: There are no edible slime recipes in this book. **Do not eat any of these slimes!**

I love being a part of the slime community and can't wait for you to be a part of it too. **Now, let's have some fun!**

INSTANT CLEAR SLIME

I can make this recipe in about one minute flat! It's so easy. Plus, there are endless modifications. It's perfect for parties, presents, and holidays.

WHAT YOU NEED

- 2 ½ oz. contact lens solution
- ½ tsp. baking soda
- 4 oz. clear PVA glue

- Small-to-medium-size mixing bowl
- Mixing utensil (spoon, silicone spatula, or craft sticks)

HERE'S HOW TO MAKE IT!

1 Pour contact lens solution into the mixing bowl.

2 Add ½ tsp. baking soda. Mix until it dissolves.

3 Pour 4 oz. clear PVA glue directly into the contact lens solution and baking soda mix. Let the glue sit in solution untouched for 5 seconds.

4 Wet your fingers with contact lens solution by dipping your hands into the bowl.

5 In the bowl, fold the slime over itself. Don't knead too aggressively, but make sure to mix up the ingredients.

6 When you feel the slime start to come together, remove it from the bowl. Instant clear slime!

MODIFICÄTION

EASTER EGG SLIME

This is so easy and adorable. I picked up foam Easter eggs at the dollar store and gently folded them in. That's it! What other dollar store modifications can you think of?

HIGHLIGHTER SLIME

Think highlighters are just for homework?
Think again. Coloring this clear slime
with a burst of neon is half the fun.

WHAT YOU NEED

- 6 oz. clear PVA glue

- ⅓ tsp. baking soda

- 2 tbsp. contact lens solution

- 1 neon, washable, nontoxic highlighter, any color

- Small-to-medium-size mixing bowl

- Mixing utensil (spoon, silicone spatula, or craft sticks)

- Rubber kitchen gloves (optional)

HERE'S HOW TO MAKE IT!

1 Pour 6 oz. clear PVA glue into the mixing bowl.

2 Add ⅓ tsp. baking soda. Mix until it dissolves.

3 Slowly add 2 tbsp. contact lens solution, 1 tbsp. at a time. Stir as you go.

4 Once the batter starts to come together, knead the slime with your hands until it's no longer sticky.

Protect the surface you are working on to make sure the highlighter doesn't stain. You can wear rubber kitchen gloves to protect your hands.

5 Now it's time to color! Take the cap off your favorite nontoxic highlighter and simply color directly onto your slime.

6 Fold the slime in on itself, being careful not to touch the highlighter fluid until it's fully absorbed.

MODIFICÄTION

MINI HIGHLIGHTER SLIME

To make multicolored mini highlighter slimes, split the clear slime into thirds. Color each third with a different highlighter. These are perfect gifts for your study buddies.

SUPER-GLOSS SLIME

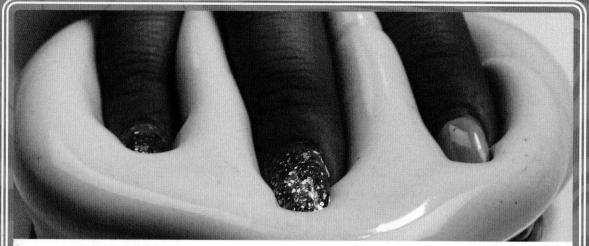

This slime is my current obsession. By adding more clear glue than white glue, you get tons of shine. And it's one of the softest, stretchiest slimes—I could play with this for hours!

WHAT YOU NEED

- 4 oz. clear PVA glue
- 3 oz. white PVA glue
- ½ tbsp. lotion*
- 1 tbsp. baby oil
- ¼ tsp. nontoxic acrylic paint
- ⅓ tsp. baking soda (about 3 pinches)

- 2–3 tbsp. contact lens solution
- Small-to-medium-size mixing bowl
- Mixing utensil (spoon, silicone spatula, or craft sticks)
- Airtight container (optional)

LET THIS RECIPE SIT OVERNIGHT FOR BEST RESULTS.

*I recommend unscented body lotion, but any lotion should work.

HERE'S HOW TO MAKE IT!

1 Pour 4 oz. clear PVA glue and 3 oz. white PVA glue into the mixing bowl.

2 Add ½ tbsp. lotion.

3 Add 1 tbsp. baby oil. Stir together with a utensil.

4 Add ¼ tsp. nontoxic acrylic paint. Stir until it is all mixed together.

I used pink paint because this color is so pretty, but you can use any color!

5 Add ⅓ tsp. baking soda. Mix until it dissolves.

6 Slowly add 2–3 tbsp. contact lens solution, 1 tbsp. at a time. Stir as you go.

7 Once the batter starts to come together, knead the slime with your hands until it's no longer sticky.

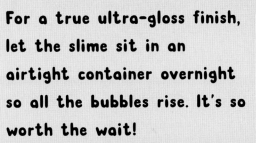

For a true ultra-gloss finish, let the slime sit in an airtight container overnight so all the bubbles rise. It's so worth the wait!

MEGA-ULTRA CRUNCH SLIME

This slime is so crunchy because air bubbles are constantly getting trapped in the straw holes. I've done an ultra-crunch slime before, but this one is even crunchier! **CRUNCHIEST. SLIME. EVER.**

WHAT YOU NEED

- 6 oz. clear PVA glue
- ⅛ to ¼ tsp. baking soda
- 1–2 tbsp. contact lens solution
- 15 clear plastic drinking straws
- 1 tbsp. foam filler beads*

- Safety scissors
- Small-to-medium-size mixing bowl
- Mixing utensil (spoon, silicone spatula, or craft sticks)
- Airtight container (optional)

☾(LET THIS RECIPE SIT OVERNIGHT FOR BEST RESULTS.

*Sold at craft stores, big box stores, and online.

HERE'S HOW TO MAKE IT

1. Pour 6 oz. clear PVA glue into the mixing bowl.

2. Add ⅛ to ¼ tsp. baking soda. Mix until it dissolves.

3. Slowly add 1 tbsp. contact lens solution. Stir as you go. 1 tbsp. should be enough for this recipe. You can add the second tbsp., a little at a time, if your slime is too sticky to come together.

You want this slime to be sticky enough to hold the straws and beads in place.

4 Once the batter starts to come together, knead the slime with your hands.

Remember, it's going to be on the sticky side.

5 Using safety scissors, carefully cut 15 drinking straws into small pieces, about ¼ inch long.

Add straw pieces and 1 tbsp. foam beads to the slime and knead them in. Sooo crunchy.

If you let this sit overnight in an airtight container, it will get more transparent and even crunchier!

CITRUS JELLY CUBE SLIME

If you're a fan of jelly slime, you'll love this fruity, squishy recipe. Sponge cubes add such a crazy texture. The longer you let this sit, the more amazing the texture gets. It's the coolest slime ever!

WHAT YOU NEED

- 10 oz. clear PVA glue
- 4 drops of food coloring
- ¼ tsp. skin-safe scent*
- ⅓ tsp. baking soda
- 2–3 tbsp. contact lens solution
- Small-to-medium-size mixing bowl
- Mixing utensil (spoon, spatula, or craft sticks)
- 2 plain sponges‡
- Safety scissors
- Rubber kitchen gloves (optional)
- Airtight container (optional)

LET THIS RECIPE SIT OVERNIGHT FOR BEST RESULTS.

*Sold at craft stores, big box stores, and online for making soaps and lotions. Use only skin-safe scents.

‡Make sure these are plain sponges without a scratchy side or added chemicals.

HERE'S HOW TO MAKE IT!

1 Pour 10 oz. clear PVA glue into the mixing bowl.

2 Add 4 drops of orange food coloring. Then mix it together with a utensil.

3 Add ⅓ tsp. baking soda. Mix until it dissolves.

4 Add ¼ tsp. orange skin-safe scent.

5

Slowly add 2–3 tbsp. contact lens solution, 1 tbsp. at a time. Stir as you go.

Protect the surface you are working on to make sure the food coloring doesn't stain. You can wear rubber kitchen gloves to protect your hands.

6

Once the batter starts to come together, knead the slime with your hands until it's no longer sticky.

7

Use safety scissors to cut 10-15 small cubes from the sponges, and add them to your slime. Don't add too many because they will soak up all of your slime.

8 Mix in the sponge cubes with your hands.

For best results, put the slime in an airtight container and let it sit for a few hours or overnight before playing with it. That will clear the slime and allow the sponges to soak it up!

MODIFICÄTION

ZOMBIE BOOGERS SLIME

Turn your fruity-smelling Citrus Jelly Cube Slime into a gross, green slime perfect for Halloween! Follow the same steps, but make a few changes. Use green food coloring instead of orange, and leave out the skin-safe scent. Use a magic eraser instead of a regular sponge. Have an adult cut the magic eraser into 5-8 small cubes, and then crush the pieces once the slime is made. See if you can work this scary slime into your next Halloween costume!

You'll need an adult to help you with this project.

SNOW CONE SLUSHIE SLIME

This one looks good enough to eat, but remember that you can't!
The good news is that you can play with Snow Cone Slime
all year round—and it doesn't melt!

WHAT YOU NEED

- 4 oz. clear PVA glue

- ¼ tsp. baking soda

- 1 tbsp. contact lens solution

- 1 drop each of red, blue, and yellow food coloring

- 5 tbsp. clear filler beads*

- Small-to-medium-size mixing bowl

- Mixing utensil (spoon, silicone spatula, or craft sticks)

- Airtight plastic container or cup

- Rubber kitchen gloves (optional)

*Sold at most craft and décor stores. These are small, hard beads made of plastic. They can be any shape, but do not get the jelly ones.

HERE'S HOW TO MAKE IT!

1 Pour 4 oz. clear PVA glue into the mixing bowl.

2 Add ¼ tsp. baking soda. Mix until it dissolves.

3 Add 1 tbsp. contact lens solution. Stir it in.

4

Once the batter starts to come together, knead the slime with your hands.

5

Add 5 tbsp. filler beads. Mix them in with your hands.

This slime will be a tad bit sticky, but that's good—you want it to be sticky so the beads stay in the slime.

Split slime into 3 equal parts. Add 1 drop of food coloring to each part. Mix together with your hands.

Protect the surface you are working on to make sure the food coloring doesn't stain. You can wear rubber kitchen gloves to protect your hands.

7

Place the three colored pieces side-by-side in a cup. Now it looks like a snow cone!

Place the slime in an airtight container and give it as a gift. It looks so cute all packaged up.

CRUSHED-DISCO BALL SLIME

This spin on slushie slime looks like a super-crunchy, crushed-up disco ball. And who doesn't want a little more sparkle in their life?

WHAT YOU NEED

- 4 oz. clear PVA glue
- ¼ tsp. baking soda
- 1 tbsp. contact lens solution
- 5 tbsp. clear filler beads*

- ½ tbsp. chunky silver glitter
- ½ tbsp. fine holographic glitter‡
- Small-to-medium-size mixing bowl
- Mixing utensil (spoon, silicone spatula, or craft sticks)

*Sold at most craft and décor stores. These are small, hard beads made of plastic. They can be any shape, but do not get the jelly ones.

‡Sold at most big box craft stores.

HERE'S HOW TO MAKE IT!

1 Pour 4 oz. clear PVA glue into the mixing bowl.

2 Add ¼ tsp. baking soda. Mix until it dissolves.

3 Add 1 tbsp. contact lens solution. Stir it in.

4 Once the batter starts to come together, knead the slime with your hands.

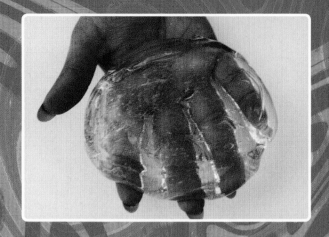

5 Add 5 tbsp. filler beads. Mix them in with your hands.

This slime will be a tad bit sticky but that's good—you want it to be sticky so the beads stay in the slime.

6 Add ½ tbsp. chunky silver glitter and ½ tbsp. fine holographic glitter.

7 Knead the glitter into the slime with your hands.

This slime looks and feels cool! So glittery! It's perfect for parties!

BUTTER SLIME

This is a super-popular type of slime, and for good reason.
It's super-soft and spreads like butter!
Playing with it is very relaxing. Just don't eat it!

WHAT YOU NEED

- 6 oz. white PVA glue

- ¼ tbsp. lotion, plus some extra*

- ¼ tsp. baking soda

- 2 tbsp. contact lens solution

- 1 oz. Daiso Japan Soft Clay‡ or any soft clay

- Small-to-medium-size mixing bowl

- Mixing utensil (spoon, silicone spatula, or craft sticks)

*I recommend unscented body lotion, but any lotion should work.

‡Sold at Daiso Japan stores and online.

HERE'S HOW TO MAKE IT!

1 Pour 6 oz. white PVA glue into the mixing bowl.

2 Add ¼ tsp. baking soda and ¼ tbsp. lotion. Mix until it dissolves.

3 Slowly add 2 tbsp. contact lens solution, 1 tbsp. at a time. Stir as you go.

4

Once the batter starts to come together, knead the slime with your hands until it's no longer sticky.

5

Mix in 1 oz. soft clay with your hands. Now you have Butter Slime!

If you used a clay other than Daiso Japan Soft Clay and the Butter Slime didn't turn out as soft as you'd like, mix in another $3/8$ tsp. lotion.

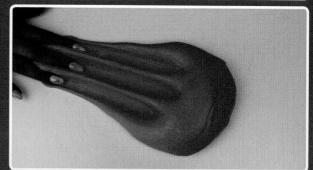

SIMPLIFIED BUTTER SLIME

Add ½ tbsp. lotion to 5 oz. soft clay and knead them together. It feels just like Butter Slime— and there's no glue involved.

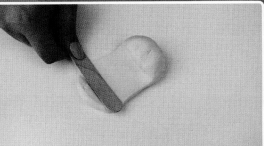

MODIFICÄTION

CANDY CANE SLIME

Make this perfect Christmas slime by adding ¼ tsp. peppermint skin-safe scent* to step 2. Once you've completed step 4, separate the batter in half. With your hands, mix in ½ oz. red clay to one half, and then ½ oz. white clay to the other half. Twist the slimes together to make a pretty candy cane swirl!

PEANUT BUTTER SLIME

To make peanut-free peanut butter slime, add ¼ tsp. peanut butter skin-safe scent* (optional) to step 2. Use brown clay in step 5. It goes great with the Jelly Slime recipe on page 42. Just don't eat it!

*Sold at craft stores, big box stores, and online for making soaps and lotions. Use only skin-safe scents.

JELLY SLIME

It's jelly time! This slime isn't edible, but mixed with peanut butter slime, it looks and smells like everybody's favorite sandwich. Yum!

WHAT YOU NEED

- 6 oz. clear PVA glue

- ⅓ tsp. baking soda (about 3 pinches)

- 3 drops of red food coloring

- 3 tbsp. contact lens solution

- 8 tbsp. water

- 1 tbsp. just-add-water instant snow powder*

- ¼ tsp. strawberry skin-safe scent‡

- 2 small-to-medium-size mixing bowls

- Mixing utensil (spoon, silicone spatula, or craft sticks)

- Airtight container (optional)

- Rubber kitchen gloves (optional)

LET THIS RECIPE SIT OVERNIGHT FOR BEST RESULTS.

*Sold at big box stores and online. It's different than plastic snow, which won't give you the same effect.

‡Sold at craft stores, big box stores, and online for making soaps and lotions. Use only skin-safe scents.

HERE'S HOW TO MAKE IT!

1 Pour 6 oz. clear PVA glue into the mixing bowl.

2 Add 3 drops of food coloring. Mix until it's distributed evenly.

3 Add ⅓ tsp. baking soda. Mix until it dissolves.

4 Stir in ¼ tsp. strawberry skin-safe scent.

Slowly add 3 tbsp. contact lens solution, 1 tbsp. at a time. Stir as you go.

6

Once the batter starts to come together, knead the slime with your hands until it's no longer sticky.

7

In a separate bowl, mix 1 tbsp. instant snow powder with 8 tbsp. water. The snow will grow.

Protect the surface you are working on to make sure the food coloring doesn't stain. You can wear rubber kitchen gloves to protect your hands.

8 Add the snow to the slime and begin mixing with your hands.

9 Continuously fold the slime over itself until the snow is evenly distributed. About two minutes of kneading and stretching should be enough.

It will be sticky at first, but it will quickly become fluffier and thicker. For best results, let the jelly slime sit in an airtight container overnight to get the air bubbles out.

MODIFICATION

PB&J SLIME

Make a sandwich with this Jelly Slime and the Peanut Butter Modification on page 41. Squishy bread toys are sold online and make these non-edible slimes look good enough to eat!

TEDDY BEAR CLOUD SLIME

This slime is so soft and fluffy, smells like chocolate, and the bow adds the most perfect teddy bear touch.

WHAT YOU NEED

- 4 oz. white PVA glue
- ¼ tsp. baking soda
- ¼ tbsp. lotion
- 1 ½ tsp. contact lens solution
- 4 tsp. just-add-water instant snow powder*
- 5 ½ tbsp. water

- 2 small-to-medium-size mixing bowls
- Mixing utensil (spoon, silicone spatula, or craft sticks)
- ½ tsp. brown nontoxic acrylic paint
- ¼ tsp. chocolate skin-safe scent ‡
- Red bow charm (optional) △

*Sold at big box stores and online. Plastic snow won't give you the same effect.

‡Sold at craft stores, big box stores, and online for making soaps and lotions. Use only skin-safe scents.

△I bought this clay charm on Etsy, but you can use any clay charm or make your own by following the instructions on page 65.

HERE'S HOW TO MAKE IT!

1 Pour 4 oz. white PVA glue into the mixing bowl.

2 Add ¼ tsp. baking soda and ¼ tbsp. lotion. Mix until it dissolves.

3 Slowly add 1 ½ tsp. contact lens solution, 1 tsp. at a time. Stir as you go.

4 Stir in ¼ tsp. chocolate skin-safe scent.

5

Stir in ½ tsp. brown acrylic paint.

6

Once the batter starts to come together, knead the slime with your hands until it's no longer sticky.

7

In a separate bowl, mix 4 tsp. instant snow powder with 5 ½ tbsp. water. Watch the snow grow before your eyes!

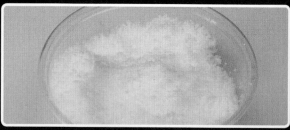

8 Add your slime to the snow bowl and begin mixing with your hands. It will be sticky at first, but it will quickly become fluffier and thicker.

9 Continuously fold the slime over itself until the snow is evenly distributed. About two minutes of kneading and stretching should be enough.

10 Optional: Add a little bow charm to officially make this Teddy Bear Cloud Slime!

MODiFiCÄTION

COTTON CANDY SLIME

To make this two-color slime, follow steps 1-3. In step 4, use cotton candy skin-safe scent* instead of chocolate. Finish the recipe, leaving out the brown paint. Then, split the slime evenly into two bowls. Add ¼ tsp. nontoxic acrylic pink paint to the first bowl, and ¼ tsp. nontoxic acrylic blue paint to the second bowl. Mix each into the Cloud Slime. Now mix slimes together to make a cotton candy swirl!

*Sold at craft stores, big box stores, and online for making soaps and lotions. Use only skin-safe scents.

CHOCOLATE TAFFY SLIME

Mirror, mirror, on the wall. Who's the thickest of them all?
This slime is so thick that it looks like chocolate taffy.
(But don't eat it—this is just for playing!)

WHAT YOU NEED

- 6 oz. Elmer's Glue-All White PVA glue*

- 1 tsp. cornstarch

- 1 ¼ tsp. lotion‡

- 1 tbsp. baby oil

- 1–2 tbsp. contact lens solution

- 1 tsp. brown acrylic paint

- ¼ tsp. chocolate skin-safe scent△

- Small-to-medium-size mixing bowl

- Mixing utensil (spoon, silicone spatula, or craft sticks)

*Thicker than regular glue, this is needed to create that taffy texture! Sold at craft and office supply stores.

‡I recommend unscented body lotion, but any lotion should work.

△Sold at craft stores, big box stores, and online for making soaps and lotions. Use only skin-safe scents.

HERE'S HOW TO MAKE IT!

1 Pour 6 oz. Elmer's Glue-All White PVA glue into the mixing bowl.

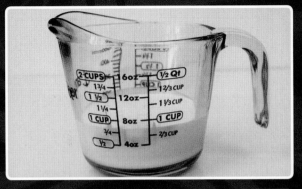

2 Stir in 1 tbsp. cornstarch to thicken up the glue even more.

3 Stir in 1 ¼ tsp. lotion with craft stick.

4 Stir in 1 tsp. baby oil for shine.

5 Stir in 1 tsp. brown acrylic paint and ¼ tsp. chocolate skin-safe scent with a craft stick.

6 Add ¼ tsp. baking soda. Mix until it dissolves.

7 Stir in up to 2 tbsp. contact lens solution, 1 tbsp. at a time. 1 tbsp. is probably enough for this recipe, but if it's still sticking, go ahead and add the second. Don't add more than that!

8 Once the batter starts to come together, knead the slime with your hands until it's no longer sticky.

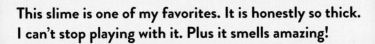

This slime is one of my favorites. It is honestly so thick. I can't stop playing with it. Plus it smells amazing!

HOLOGRAPHIC SLIME

This slime is the coolest holo slime ever, hands down!
It's made with a special powdered nail pigment that makes it
look incredibly holographic-almost like an oil spill.

WHAT YOU NEED

- 6 oz. clear PVA glue

- ⅓ tsp. baking soda (about 3 pinches)

- 2 tbsp. contact lens solution

- ¼ tsp. holographic powdered nail pigment*

- Small-to-medium-size mixing bowl

- Mixing utensil (spoon, silicone spatula, or craft sticks)

*Sold at beauty supply stores and big box stores. FYI, holographic glitter won't work as well as powdered nail pigment.

HERE'S HOW TO MAKE IT!

1 Pour 6 oz. clear PVA glue into the mixing bowl.

2 Add ⅓ tsp. baking soda. Mix until it dissolves.

3 Slowly add 2 tbsp. contact lens solution, 1 tbsp. at a time. Stir as you go.

4 Once the batter starts to come together, knead the slime with your hands until it's no longer sticky.

5 Add ¼ tsp. nail pigment powder. Mix in with your hands.

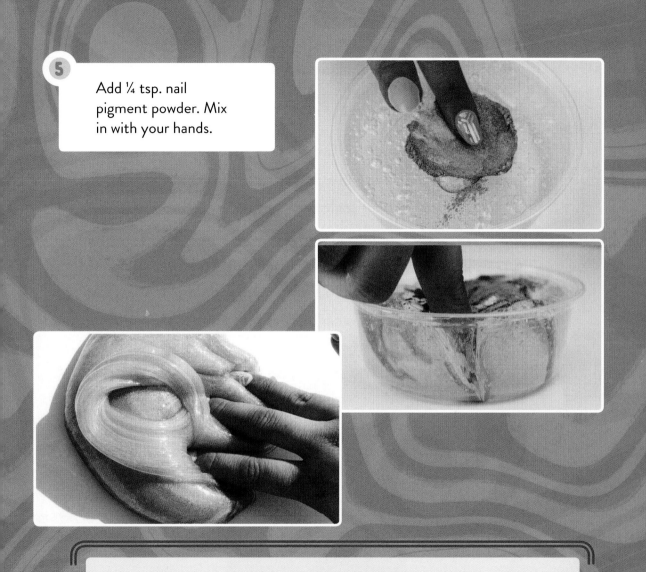

Shine a light onto your slime.
It should look so rainbow-y and holographic!

MODIFICATION

COLOR-CHANGING SLIME

To make this slime, follow the same steps but make a few substitutions. Use ¼ tsp. baking soda instead of ⅓ tsp. Add ½ tsp. color-changing pigment* instead of ¼ tsp. holographic pigment. Now you have a whole different slime! My slime turns light green when I hold it, but different pigments work differently. Make sure to read the instructions on your pigment.

*Skin-safe, heat-activated, color-changing pigment is available online and in some craft stores.

CEREAL SLIME

You'll need an adult to help you with this project.

Make your own marshmallow-like charms for this milky slime.
Warning: Sadly, this is not edible!
But it does look like a real breakfast treat.

WHAT YOU NEED

- 3 oz. white PVA glue
- 3 oz. clear PVA glue
- ¼ tsp. baking soda
- ¼ tbsp. lotion
- 2 tbsp. contact lens solution
- ¼ tsp. cereal skin-safe scent*

- Baking clay
- Clay tools
- Plastic beads (optional)
- Small-to-medium-size mixing bowl
- Mixing utensil (spoon, silicone spatula, or craft sticks)
- Airtight container

*Cereal skin-safe scents are hard to find, but can be found online.
Vanilla scent is a good substitute. Use only skin-safe scents.

HERE'S HOW TO MAKE IT!

1 Pour 3 oz. white PVA glue and 3 oz. clear PVA glue into the mixing bowl.

A mix of white and clear PVA glue gives it a super-glossy, milk-like look.

2 Add ¼ tsp. baking soda and ¼ tbsp. lotion. Mix until it dissolves.

3 Slowly add 2 tbsp. contact lens solution, 1 tbsp. at a time. Stir as you go.

4

Add ¼ tsp. of your favorite cereal skin-safe scent. Stir with a craft stick.

I chose a scent that mimics the scent of Lucky Charms cereal.

5

Once the batter starts to come together, knead the slime with your hands until it's no longer sticky.

6

Set your slime base aside in an airtight container and get ready for the next step: making charms!

7 Roll baking clay into a ball, roll or flatten it, and then use clay-cutting utensils to cut out the cereal shapes. I made rainbows!

8 With help from an adult, bake in an oven according to the directions on the package. When finished, let it cool completely.

9 Now add the clay charms to your slime.

10 Optional: Add plastic beads in the shape of your favorite cereal to make this slime look— and smell—so real!

MERMAID DREAM FISHBOWL SLIME

Hold a piece of the ocean in your hands. Shimmering, shiny, so pretty!

WHAT YOU NEED

- 4 oz. clear PVA glue
- ⅛ to ¼ tsp. baking soda
- 1 drop each of blue and green food coloring
- 1–2 tbsp. contact lens solution
- 1–2 cups fishbowl beads*
- 1 fake gold leaf sheet‡
- Small-to-medium-size mixing bowl
- Mixing utensil (spoon, silicone spatula, or craft sticks)
- Rubber kitchen gloves (optional)
- Clay charms (optional), glitter, or gems△

*Flat, round acrylic beads sold at craft stores in the floral arrangement section.

‡Used to decorate crafts. It's sold at craft stores in the painting section.

△I bought these clay charms on Etsy, but you can use any clay charms or make your own by following the instructions on page 65.

HERE'S HOW TO MAKE IT!

1 Pour 4 oz. clear PVA glue into the mixing bowl.

2 Add in 1 drop of blue and 1 drop of green food coloring. Stir well.

3 Add ¼ tsp. baking soda. Mix until it dissolves.

4 Slowly add 1–2 tbsp. contact lens solution, 1 tbsp. at a time. Stir as you go.

Protect the surface you are working on to make sure the food coloring doesn't stain. You can wear rubber kitchen gloves to protect your hands.

5 Once the batter starts to come together, knead the slime with your hands until it's no longer sticky.

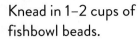

6 Knead in 1–2 cups of fishbowl beads.

7 Now add the gold leaf sheet to your slime. It's super-cool because it breaks into pieces and is so fun to mix in.

8 Optional: If you want to be even more mermaid-y, finish by kneading in some additional clay charms, glitter, or gems.

CANDLE SLIME

You'll need an adult to help you with this project.

Got a favorite scented candle? Turn it into slime!
It smells so good and the texture is totally unique.

WHAT YOU NEED

- ½ cup wax from a candle
- 8 oz. white PVA glue
- ¼ tsp. baking soda
- 1 tbsp. acrylic paint
- 1 ¼ tsp. lotion*

- 2–3 tbsp. contact lens solution
- Small-to-medium-size heat-safe mixing bowl (like glass)
- Mixing utensil (spoon, silicone spatula, or craft sticks)
- Oven mitts

*I recommend unscented body lotion, but any lotion should work.

HERE'S HOW TO MAKE IT!

1 Ask an adult to light a wax candle and let it melt completely. After blowing out the candle, let it stand for 1 minute to cool the wax slightly. The wax should still be liquid.

2 Ask an adult who is wearing oven mitts to pour about ½ cup of melted wax from the candle into a heat-safe glass bowl.

3 While the wax is still liquid, pour 8 oz. white PVA glue and 1 tbsp. acrylic paint into the mixing bowl.

4 Add ¼ tsp. baking soda and 1 ¼ tsp. lotion. Mix until it dissolves.

5 Slowly add 2–3 tbsp. contact lens solution, 1 tbsp. at a time. Stir as you go.

6 Stir until the batter starts to come together. Once all the wax has hardened, knead the slime with your hands until it's no longer sticky.

Never touch liquid wax. It could be hot! When the wax is fully cooled and safe to touch, it'll be solid and give your slime a grainy texture.

I made two batches of candle slime and mixed them together to get this cool look!

PLAYING WITH, CLEANING, AND PRESERVING SLIME

Playing with Slime

Okay, so you can do whatever you want when it comes to slime. There are no real rules, but if you poke a certain slime that shouldn't be poked, it makes slimers cringe. Here are some of the unspoken rules of the slime community.

• **Butter Slime:** Spread it like butter! Place it on a table and smooth it around with your hands. Then fold it onto itself and repeat.

• **Glossy Slime:** Place it on a table and poke it with your fingertips. Pulling, clicking, popping, and folding are okay, too.

• **Crunchy Slime:** Grab it between your hands, then squeeze, stretch, and fold!

• **Cloud Slime:** Stretch and fold it back and forth between your hands to create lines. Then make it into a swirl on a table. No poking allowed! It doesn't make any noise.

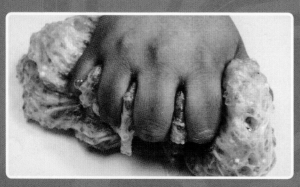

More Ways to Play

There are so many creative ways to play with slime. Here are just a few of my favorites.

• Put it in a **balloon** and make a stress ball. Different textures of slime will give you different-feeling stress balls. I've made giant stress balls out of mesh on my YouTube channel.

• Press it into the head of a **tennis racket** or through a strainer to make bubbles appear and to add textures to your slime.

• Put it through a **pasta maker** to stretch it out. Make sure the slime doesn't have beads or solid pieces.

Cleaning Up Slime

Whenever I'm on tour, I get super-excited when a fan gives me a package of slime. I open it right then and there and start poking it. But then when I go onstage later, I always have slime on my clothes! When slime sinks into carpeting or clothing, here's what you do:

1. Have a grown-up cover the slime with citric acid powder.

2. Wait at least 1 minute.

3. Scrub out the slime.

Citric acid literally melts the slime!

You can follow the same steps using white vinegar, but let it sit for a few minutes before scrubbing out the slime.

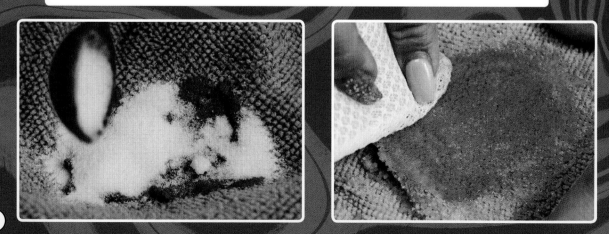

Preserving Slime

The best way to store your slime is in a sealed container in a cool place or somewhere that is at least room temperature. A plastic food jar or container will do, as long as it's airtight. In the summer when it gets really hot, slime can melt. If this happens, pop your slime in the freezer for an hour or two and it will be good as new.

Over time, slime does start to lose its texture, but a little activator can fix it. I always keep extra activator (baking soda and contact lens solution) on hand. That way, I'm always ready to make slime or breathe some life into some old slime.

FAN SLIMES

People give me so much slime. It's the best! I always want to start playing with it. These are some of the most memorable slimes I've received. Thank you to everyone who has given me slime—y'all are amazing!

Karina Slime

One fan gave me clear slime that had tiny, laminated photos of myself inside of it. It was incredible!

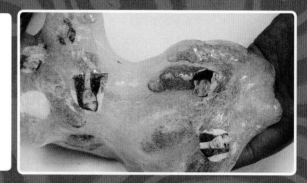

Early Cloud Slime

A fan gave me cloud slime before it was a big thing, and I thought it was so cool. I'm always amazed at how creative the slime community is. Now, cloud slime is so popular!

Slime with Peanut Butter

This slime had actual peanut butter in it. I loved it so much, but within days, it rotted. I figured out a way to make a peanut butter and jelly-inspired slime on page 45 that will last a lot longer.

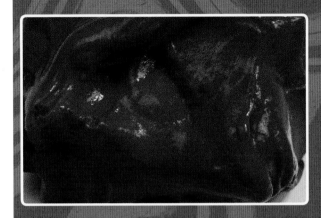

Giant Slime

The slimers from *Life with Brothers* on YouTube had bought something like 20 of my slime kits and made giant blobs of slime out of them. I couldn't believe it!

ABOUT THE AUTHOR

Karina Garcia is a DIY and overall lifestyle expert with a wildly popular YouTube channel watched by over 7 million subscribers, two best-selling books, and a crafting product line, Craft City, available exclusively at Target. She is considered to be one of the most followed crafters on the internet.

Beyond sharing slime recipes and other creative crafts with the world, Karina loves design, style, and keeping up with the latest trends. She's appeared on programs such as *Good Morning America*, *The Ellen DeGeneres Show*, and *The Today Show*, and has been featured in numerous publications, such as the *New York Times*.

To learn more, follow Karina on social media:

YouTube: /TheKarinaBear

Instagram: @karinagarc1a

Twitter: @Karinaa_Bear

ALSO BY KARINA GARCIA: